COMMON PLACE

COMMON PLACE

SARAH PINDER

COACH HOUSE BOOKS | TORONTO

first edition

Published with the generous assistance of the Canada Council for the Arts and the Ontario Arts Council. Coach House Books also acknowledges the support of the Government of Canada through the Canada Book Fund and the Government of Ontario through the Ontario Book Publishing Tax Credit.

LIBRARY AND ARCHIVES CANADA CATALOGUING IN PUBLICATION

Pinder, Sarah, 1983-, author
        Common place / Sarah Pinder.

A poem.
Issued in print and electronic formats.
ISBN 978-1-55245-346-9 (softcover).

        I. Title.

PS8631.I5IC66 2017   C811.6   C2017-900536-7

Common Place is available as an ebook: ISBN 978 1 77056 513 5 (EPUB), ISBN 978 1 77056 514 2 (PDF).

COMMON PLACE

□

Tumbling behind pleasure
on our best behaviour,
holding its hands.

The sweeter version:
hollow, ropey, and roaring,
in redux with the truest reds.

Step by step, man in a blue suit,
man with a baby, man kneading the grass,
carrying some matte black apparatus.

Digging the trough for a headstone,
a fleshy neutrality of debt, lymph-tinted.

You can't pay back flicker –
we're in marked space, using
our bottle caps to place
three-minute video calls home.

□

Kid on a gas-powered low-rider,
tearing up the middle of the potholed street,

arcs wide at the end of the block,
his unexpected giggling passing
a third time,

shooting into the pointillist pinks,
engine spluttering.

Barely a sidewalk,
barely a fence to walk through.

□

Yes, they are real.
No, we didn't kill them,
but we did dip them in lacquer
to make them our own.

Yes, you have debts, and we've moved
beyond administrative whispers,
toward the ploughing under.

On the other side of time, spun up,
you will not remember
why she dragged
the bed into the yard,
lit it on fire.

Who can really remember?
The past is a mould.

Wrapped boxes eventually shrink.
Cables and bottles of urine move
into your car on the other side of time,
corroding slowly.

Pallets of remote control
monster trucks, antennae bowed.

Make a gift of your boxes of flatware,
sheers, appliances that dice – whatever
you give, give in
sets of matching sets.

Make a gift of your violence.

□

It's probably not dead, but it gets quiet
at the end of the street.

I walked backwards to get here.
Things grew in reverse, the halls were ornamented
in plaster birds, butterflies, and moths
sequentially preening themselves.

In the summer of ruins,
parked behind the hotel,
air was thickest after the trees,
near the refinery.

There was no record
and then her script carved through,
unmourned and so damned demanding.

□

The way I remember houses is empty
but with television on American news
elevatedly announcing the broad, low
part of the afternoon.

We should spread that risk around a bit.

□

Casual trauma keeps meticulous records,
keeps itself real cool
in a snowsuit in perforated photo books,
in a straw hat and bathing suit at the strip of beach
along the new highway still smelling of money,
in white hot pants with white go-go
boots and a well-closed cape,
twice inscribed.

Joy, a movement
sped into after-images.

In the crowd, animals tremble,
tongue the air, loosen.

For my dearth, I have often been parchment.
I am low growing, with caustic taste.

A clot of hair in the storm drain
at the entrance to the necropolis,
marbled middle of the grid,
stadium lights across the tracks,
mercenarylike.

I walked with you here, hastily.
Lesser, somewhat.

I recall the bell of your mouth
marked with gold lines,
as if scored.

□

From a local name for ginko,
from San Francisco, packed in
biodegradable foam chips,
an epithet that translates to: useless,
ash.

Teeth are originally thought to have
developed from scales covering the lips.

The book about the ground-out city
shows its claws so kindly,
waving a battery tealight around.

Behind the book, there is ankle-deep water
from a small fountain coughing up
through the floor.

Behind this video is a farm owner in Greece
who shot twenty-eight Bangladeshi labourers
demanding to be paid at all
for months of strawberries.

      Broke them short, then walked
                    into acquittal.

The sun is lion's tooth,
lion's tail, shredding flowers.

□

Every day, I am governed,
even in a private tonguing
or while retching,
wreathing the toilet with interiors
or running in the service lanes,
feeling the unpredictable
jiggle of my thighs
driven toward accounting.

Walking the cruising paths
in long sleeves that could be stripped off,
wading in the neutrality of the shade,
understudied but awake.

The fuzzed shoreline,
beach pea swallowing up the dunes.

□

We position ourselves as guests
when it suits us.

□

Flowering fig,
fruit pecked by sparrows.

All in sugar or in syrup,
in honey or olive oil.

In distilled water,
in brine,
in blood.

□

We were eager to stand in
order in the public square,
which was private,
to bring our publics
to face the same direction.

□

A woman moves and there are curved elations
in her relationship to existing leanness.

There are costs to having personal history,
and ideals require aggregate and throb.

If you go to your balcony in the evening,
there will be a feeling that the city has shorted out.

□

We are trying to keep the moment
when the worst seems to have
not happened.

Standing together, we were an amphitheatre
pulling on our clear masks.
It was said to be safer that way.
The sweat ran sunblock into our eyes.

When told the worst has not happened,
citizens try to follow.

In clouded night,
with a knee bend that some interpret as richness,
when walking with a whitish bloom,
or drawing out diagrams,
scratching through pictures of the sun,
in analogue.

I wanted to do some work each day,
even if it was just holding the lid
on the box a little longer.

□

Spine and spine – that whole business
butted up against the kitchen counter,
head forced into the sink – they were
certainly on my mind as much as the dead.

□

We brought insolvency to the wedding,
carried it to the church
we were baptized in,
        danced
                in the hall and were fed, drank together,
                took home their flower arrangements
                when we left.

□

Lit her own dress up,
nylon into acrid sap.

Hare-like through the picture
window and bloody
on the droughted lawn

One cut crystal tumbler
through which artificial
light passes.

□

A beautiful pink line flutters
on the side of my screen,
back to forth.

☐

Let's keep mineral pigments in here.

Is there room for two bodies in this story:
the unquenchable thirst of one, the long dry feeling
of its neighbour, cuticle stripping, taking classes
to learn confinement techniques from men
we wish we would not learn these things from,
weaving bleary through the subway,
going home?

Letters come on foolscap in monitored relations.
Is there room for an audience in here,
even though there are no chairs?

Is there room for crossing the streetcar tracks
on an angle with thin wheels, every bump
and gap humming between your legs?
For tacking back to pick up a handwritten list,
barely legible,
to photograph that list instead of pocket it,
then return it to the sidewalk.

The sleek body of a cat appearing middle frame,
interested in your crouching
observation and outstretched hand.

□

The months I gathered no flowers,
touched no confection,
drank quiet water, warm as a wrist,
no warmer.

□

Slipping loose of the subject to dart to the fence line
        and hide
                under flowering crab, tail coiled.

□

His ink-stained shirt front hidden in linen,
the man I read in the capital with, in a mouldering room
full of paintings by separatists.

He wanted a photo.

I played a woman in the picture
taken by his son.

I was trying to be an obelisk.

He did nothing unusual, touched me
          with a familiarity I always lose in.

□

Forced falls neaten
when ringed
by velvet rope.

The galaxy
of a fat bruise
tears through rich
order.

In the audience's tourism,
they keep in mind a country
undeclared, not to be
spoken of, turn
their single face
toward the mountain
and try to seep in.

□

Another yellow room where I start to paint
over bruises, trying something further from skin.

□

Land around the new shoots:
garbage bags torn open,
blouses pooled out.

□

We have a longing – it is not dead,
but it is very quiet.

Cadillac passes and a melancholic
man shouts things at our sheened body.

We still covet the night
running in circles.

Two young boys in flip-flops
dance in the dust,
kick wildly to bring up clouds.

□

Split shift heredity,

>phantom hours,
>bull-headed
>in the beautiful mint.

Keep me from slipping
while I rattle for a while
>in the weight of static,
coin quietly clinking.

□

Still good, just marked
with still lines.

□

If, then, on the same property
I no longer see.

If, then, to be the same property
now, or to have been,

as though I was at first soft moss,
coming away in clumps.

□

In the elevator to the dressing room,
　　　clutching a stranger's shoulders.

In the mall, an anchorite
　　　meditating on the unbagged quality of light.

　　Glory, glory.

Unzipping our dresses in the washroom
to trace the places we'd marked
ourselves,
　　　learn they nearly matched.

□

Pool pumps humming thick
liquid of pre-dawn cul-de-sac.

        Drought summer,
        we hoard our water,
        keep it
                tiled blue.

□

Gasoline, jet fuel, home heating oil,
diesel, ammonia,
sewage.

Drinking water organized
somewhat differently.

□

Keep stamping the ledger.

I want to learn the names of things that grow here.

>   No ascetic vision,
>   just stubborn rush,
>   a pack of dollar-store sewing needles,
>   alcohol evaporating on skin.

□

Crooked crayon,

        junk-picked yellow slide
        strapped down to the trailer.

Taking blurry portraits
on the runway,

        cropping out the nose and mouth.

Portraits at the self-storage
after eleven,

        with the faintest idea
        of beacons.

Portraits under the overpass
with small depressions,

        shirtless in the ragweed
        but for a washed-out red bra.

□

Wild mustard, metrics of implied inferiority
not required, but why does it matter?

We run backwards away
anyway.

A woman burning a mattress in the yard
is not private, but we desperately want to be
private,

two girls whispering in blackberry
cane at the rifle range.

□

At the river mouth, throwing rocks
to delight her baby,
who wants to kiss the smooth stones
before we send them into the moment,
to kiss each leaf,
     all the way
        up the bank.

Wending through the valley,
     passing each farm
     against progress, the mountain –

the baby cries
and the best solution is to sing
together.

The ferry arrives to pull us across:
we cut our engines, the cable slips
back into the water to keep the boat true.

□

Make it froth and try –
tongue, too,
smacked,
swallowing.

□

I call you state,
you call me city.

Swing the trinkets
every time you punch out.

Text me again from the hill
behind the community centre
or the dry riverbed,
half of where you are
on fire, as is common this season.

□

One quick slap on a side street,
tights abruptly down,
then off again,
walking, not running.

□

Is gold leaf or a cast claw money?

Fox jaw continues to sing, but sings a new song.
Won't shut up.

Can we say that we are still with us?
We have our somnambulism for our fitness.
We said we could not be adapted more.

□

I was a crow skirting the outer bodies
with a hair in my mouth,
meticulously prepared.

Or I was an ox rib in the bone shed,
thinking stone boat, atone –

□

I had a long look out
the window – muddy below
nearly white sky cut up
by scaffolding, then into the sleeve
of the city again,
tunnelview and crush,
emptying core.

□

A feature about the citizens of a place
for citizens to watch
in the peeling theatre, blanketed
with overactive heat.

□

People who didn't live in the neighbourhood
took photos when demolition began,
admiring the colour of each cube
as the facing wall of the complex
came down.

□

Work and, without waking,
flex everything
to keep it blank
like any other
receiver, just stay happy
and upgraded,
barely thinking,
stay a lover who spits up
what you are wanting
into the sink.

□

Before it had been absent, it was a task,
water ready to empty.

I was absent in the tension
throughout my body.

I didn't discuss it.

When I got to Chicago,
I kept splitting into quarters,
then eighths.

Fingering waistbands,
bag checked and a playing card
slipped in my back pocket.

Five of diamonds
laminated with packing tape.

□

Let me be
sure I understand
what you are
communicating:
do not be afraid.

In the dim gallery rooms
on benches, then the floor, trying
to find the exact centre of the place,
my foot suddenly sluggish,
wrists sparkling.

◻

A clearing:
thumbing torn leaves.

Right now,
when my name is just mine,
sharpened and wiped
with the rag.

□

Dipping crane, keep gleaning
my perfumed hair shaken out.

Half-cover your mouth in the selfsame way
as a sentence's soft undulation.

I know you live in stadium bleed-over,
synchronizing claps through the chemicals.

I know it's your dusk, hours after mine
came on, syrupy and luxuriant.

□

Walking the shoreline
with storyteller's remorse,
which goes chattering on
along the back of your windowpanes.

You knew how to pick quartz
and had forgotten:
they drop softly to the bottom of pockets,
make the cloth fall in points.

□

Today, a week before the equinox,
and you are a tissue-paper dandelion,
the first golden herald of spring.

□

Slept in the car last night
with the smallest pen knife
hung beside me,
not even a locking blade.

Woke at five, damp, ten percent
battery and your threads
of messages,
possum slinking across
the back fence,
setting the acacia rippling.

□

Co-moving in mutual systems of transport,
tension through checkpoints, but an overall ease
facilitated by my white skin,
work that sounds federal,
                          federal sounds
misreported,
thrust off into cool salt bloom.

□

No brackets, new routes,
the tender place my fist lies
before it tells you the truth.

□

On the bus in the wrong direction,
the hospital opposite these outskirts,
the cloistered part, spun with inheritances,
prison across from recovery house.

□

Whenever I expect you,
don't expect ceremony

but shining
imitation,

stinking
with attention.

□

I don't want to trade pictures
of your bachelor suite above the barbershop
for my bachelor suite beside the women's gym.

Last time, you upped the resolution
to read my screens and papers,
and still had a wife and a list of options.

Neighbours cursing through the swamp-box,
lashes tethered to white lightning, mundane aches:
almond grove, orange grove, rapeseed, rice.

□

Really dedicated to the middle managerial
and its papers and letters, words work
with and without being opaline,
expert description singing out the loudest,
judgment adjusting its laces.

□

Any raft
leans with numbers
when drifting out.

□

If I imagine being pinned down
as though a solid conclusion is not
just possible, but anticipated,
an anti-anthem swells out of my pores.

This is what I mean
when I tell you failure is fine,
shivering is another form of document.

The recollection of your sweat
in the most uncommon
close theatres is an acid on intimacy.

I want all my limbs
whispering,
boats away from the coast.

Like speech balloons descending,
I move slowly,
dance for the mirror
with its hairline crack.

□

Filing toward the back
exit of discipline,
her phone erupts,
a bitter line that draws itself
right through this inconvenience,
the thread over your lips.

I operate as a sequence of explosions
you could lose the origin of
in your coin purse.

I have this prayer I say to myself
or to no one in particular:
'*Let me be a grey bowl,
let me be a wave.*'

□

Awake in the green room,
flat out on bedsprings,
dried milkweed tacked
to the wall, refusing any
emergency before slipping
keys in mail slots.

The plasticity of early winter,
back to the river, face to the river,
side of my body to the river,
on my way to you.

□

I wore so many layers when we met
and drank doubles, which destines me to say CAPITALISM
again and again like a more diligent newspaper Marxist,
but I did it anyway, pulled the glow on us.

I had bills with a satin feel,
had to count them through usual talk –
someone making a faggot joke at the bar,
then the long way to the station,
veneered around each others' edges,
occupying surfaces to make them
closer to parallel than overlap.

□

In an inbox or a third-hand
photocopy – sourceless
fantasy of a neutral visitor,

                    occupying.

□

The plan she showed me –

cancer again, before forgetting.

Pardon?

Cancer before the money comes down,

not raining, the way
the lottery or the pension
man says, but as the barest idea
of fog.

□

Windowless concrete promises
with sno-cone facades
diving backwards into
dead water, clear right
down to empty bottom.

□

We looked for tooth marks
on the Plexiglas sound wall,
a gnawed margin
or even an edge.

□

Ashes swept
into black tea,
only a bit
on the rim,

still, bless all
tension, bless the story
in how I slept this year,
inconstant, trained
to the tracks
and their sudden oncoming.

□

Good kitten, you said,
swinging unpredictable
with the table leg,

fucking slut,
delicious little thing,
your eyes through
sweat-wet hair,

yelling at me to pull over
in the half-ploughed lane
to snap faded purple
initials cancelled out for

ever an ever.

□

When stirred into reverse,
my violet flares are activated
and begin to stream
in a way that is often misread
as pleasant.

◻

First-person voice and thought
are uncomfortable.

What you propose is to occupy this take
and be taught by me, a type of woman, to become
somewhat more sensitive.

You've got no idea where the heat will go
but still want to keep me around.

□

I did not remember the shirt I woke up in,
and it was a surprising navy,
sleeve seams gutted to yaw.

My arms emerged
and they were possibly not my arms,
either – not the ones I went to sleep with.

Two sirens passed, twinning
before falling back into syncopation.

□

In the alley, I bent down
and touched the tip
of my tongue
to pollen
on the pavement
to take an account.

□

The banner we made from a bed sheet,
the quilt we made from work clothes
when we thought the economy changed
because we left the halls
we said it happened in.

□

Dicing fifty pounds of onions –
who pulled
       those onions from the soil?

Men in the vinegar vats,
       overcome by fumes.

□

Fronds, flowers
from a bucket,
their leaves falling
on the sidewalk
while I hold
the rubber band.

□

The subway is held at the station
but the driver sweeps his gloved hand
out the window in a benediction,
so I get on.

Once you open yourself to the utility of anger,
it comes on as fluid
looking for any channel to pull it further along.
We are above ground again, passing
through various aspects of the afternoon.

The man beside me flexes each swollen finger,
then tries to make a fist,
shakes his head, and straightens his arm,
trying to give himself some distance.

□

The more psychoanalysis
I read, the more I hold out
treats or nouns and call them signs.

□

I had a debt before.

        Now, I don't know.

But that second debt, or the third one,

        put them in the Crown Royal bag,
        draw the gold cord and swing it overhead
        faster and faster, until it disappears.

Bring me lip-first in,
        bring me right to the doorstep.

Shake it and shout,
sweet teeth,
tear the old ones from me.

□

The lesser, lower-case subject is

What do you hoard?

Is it convenient?

□

When they couldn't be left fluttering,
if they didn't run from their tethers
in gowns across the parking lot,
we tried to detach from our ownings,
carted them into dumpsters
to burn or bury the last
hospital summer.

□

Sweet shredder
of front pieces,
book by naked book,
new collections
stacked on boxes over you,
the box above.

□

If you can't do great things,
do the slightest things with flourish.

A clutch of balloons shuffles again
and again against a guard rail.

Alarms somewhere, coming on.

☐

*Tell us how you have prevented an accident
to yourself or someone else.*

Does remembrance mean anything to you?

What resolution have you made and broken?

Roll call:

Roll call:

Roll call:

□

To sing,
afterwards,
more than once,
twice –
shocked
to sing
with precision,
a clipped circuit.

I wiped my hands
on a thick lilac, my pants,
and walked with a thorn
in my perfumed knee,
a loan until later, the same logic
as life.

□

Ashed out, lace-backed,
vibrating along, soaked,
just soaked, one foot
always still
set to run.

Ulnar ache in the morning,
a bruise on my thigh
where I punched
into each coda.

□

In one of my dreams,
pulling out eye teeth
sharp as blades of grass.

□

Come on, kind night,
over the institutional pile,
my body will not float
much more,
come on, new gods,
palm my cheeks,
cup my crown, this time,
map me.

□

Flies in the vinegar,
flies in the plum wine.

□

Landslip, ease
in locked soil,
swanned out.

□

Waves, then wave
repeater, I form cursive.
I can make a cure into a vessel.

Alerts keep coming – each device
has its own way of singing out value.

Tell me what to do in this
period of secondary qualities.

I get letters from the interior
and it takes months to know
how to write back.

□

Imagine a hole in the middle of your occupations.
Mine shows a pile of bleach-blown linens
shot through with supernovas.

I don't feel sorry.
I can't feel particularly apologetic,
but I wish an accident of silence
would leave a crack down the side of this time.

Cups eject into pieces off the shelves,
great, weird flocks pass in formation
over the oily water and bone-smooth Styrofoam.

I collect sand-caked lighters instead of shells
and arrange them in a spectrum by colour.

The wedding party prepares –
a tent goes up,
the tour bus passes,
and capital continues.

This morning,
I read about a woman hollowing
out a bagel to consume the shell
stuffed with processed whiteness
and mass-smoked flesh.

I think of gusto,
sand in the crotch of your pants,
in the folds of your skin.
The tour bus passes.

I pledge to eat the crumb cake
national project at the ceremony,
scrape off the lavender icing florets first.

I try to will on rain.

□

No curb or streetlight pressure.

I'll come back to the marble
atrium pluralities, but not now –
it's time for devotion's seed pod
to be in hand.

I keep listening, sincere
at the back of the hall,
hauling myself up through
the divination deck.

Silence is preferable,
my suit of arcane texts sways.
Praise tends the archive,
accumulating handprints
in paint or blood.

Smoking in front of the open stove,
I think of watching you.

□

Where did you get those
dreamy contusions?

□

Render a citizenship,

>   absent documents
>   lost in a church fire
>   blazed through snow,
>   she said.

(Bankrupt certification.)

Proofs to provide of origin
through the turnstile,
as a stranger in a fenced line,
moved to the middle
of the latest mooring.

Self-portrait as a handful of clippings,
self-portrait as my mother's
stepmother, a stranger
working the psychiatric ward,
those people
moved to the middle,
moved away.

□

As of this writing,
the death
of a death
tracking around
my own
outside,
asking again.

□

Quick sketch of hares:

we met on a spit in winter,
unemployed, dangled
our feet over.

It was a hardening period,
some bliss sown through it

from the stomach,
the hungry lungs.

□

In the wattage of the pre-owned superstore
I am aware of other radiants, our prescriptions,
while I push the cart, one wheel
dragging with a clot of dust.

What comes after longing?
What I didn't expect:
a sixty-second clock
that restarts itself.

□

I have a bureaucratic calm I can access
from standing in the weeds across the road.

There, packing the damned thing with salt,
I sew with the cleanest stitches.

Last night, coyotes called to each other,
softening the edges of this story in their throats.

Today, through the doors, a state holiday
wrings the language.

I have no coins, I have no messages
but your last about thinning little lettuces.

I have no work
but this task.

Notes

p. 79: The line 'tear the old ones from me' is a slight revision of a phrase from *Disavowals, or Cancelled Confessions*, Claude Cahun, translated by Susan de Muth (MIT Press, 2007, p. 199). This text came my way via the Worriers song 'The Only Claude That Matters.'

p. 84: All text on this page is from the Algoma Centre District Women's Institute 1969–70 logbook.

p. 85: The last line of this section is a rehashing of 'a loan holds the same logic as life,' from *Artemidorus' Oneirocritica: Text, Translation, and Commentary*, Daniel E. Harris-McCoy (Oxford University Press, 2012, p. 281).

Acknowledgements

Sections of this book have appeared in *CV2*, The Rusty Toque, and *Carousel*.

Funds from an Ontario Arts Council Writer's Works in Progress grant allowed me time to work on this manuscript.

Thanks to Alana Wilcox, Jeramy Dodds, Norman Nehmetallah, and everyone at Coach House for working magic.

Joan Guenther, Mat Laporte, Daniel Marrone, Concetta Principe, Yosefa Raz, and Jessalyn Wakefield gave crucial feedback on early drafts.

Thanks to Miranda Bouchard; Jason Burton; Lauren Corman; Lauren, Laoh, and Sawyer Grace; Guin Kellam; Shannon Maguire; melannie monoceros; Lida Nosrati; Merrick Pilling; Cris Renna; Chy Ryan Spain; and Kate Wilson, for the conversations that brought me here.

Jennifer Nelson and Sue Sinclair gave me their generous attention. I'm grateful for it.

Encountering works by Anne Boyer, Traci Matlock, Fred Moten, and Postcommodity were formative to writing this book, as was seeing Alejandro Cartagena's remarkable *Fragmented Cities* photo essay. Thanks to Alejandro for granting permission to use one of the images from that series on the cover.

The beautiful pink line belongs to Yosefa Raz.

Sean H. Doyle made a pact with me in the summer of 2016 that helped me finish this.

Daniel Marrone – twin, I'm braver because of you.

Deepest thanks to Robert and Pamela Pinder, and to my chosen family and friends. I love you. I'm so lucky.

About the Author

Sarah Pinder lives in Toronto. She is the author of *Cutting Room*.

Typeset in Aragon.

Printed at Coach House on bpNichol Lane in Toronto, Ontario, on Zephyr Antique Laid paper, which was manufactured, acid-free, in Saint-Jérôme, Quebec, from second-growth forests. This book was printed with vegetable-based ink on a 1973 Heidelberg KORD offset litho press. Its pages were folded on a Baumfolder, gathered by hand, bound on a Sulby Auto-Minabinda and trimmed on a Polar single-knife cutter.

Edited by Jeramy Dodds
Designed by Norman Nehmetallah
Cover photo: Alejandro Cartagena, *Suburbia Mexicana*, 2006–2010.

Coach House Books
80 bpNichol Lane
Toronto ON M5S 3J4
Canada

416 979 2217
800 367 6360

mail@chbooks.com
www.chbooks.com